This book is dedicated to our Moms

CONTENTS

Preface
America's Financial Problem: Let's Unite and Take Control

Let's face it, there's a financial problem in America. And in today's tense world, we need a solution more than ever. That's where I come in. You can call me Charity, and I have a code that can end all the division. It's not a secret code, but rather a code hidden in plain sight - our tax code. Specifically, tax code 664.

I was born in the late sixties, just around the time Congress created tax code 664 in 1969, I witnessed a lot of change. Free love and hippiness were in the air for some. But my no-nonsense mother wasn't having any of it. She loved working. She wanted to be out in the world, not stuck at home. Back then, women weren't yet allowed to have their own credit cards or control their own finances. It's crazy to think about! But that didn't stop her from wanting to have control of her own money! Fortunately and Ironically she went to work for our government, in the Department of Social Security.

It's no accident that financial literacy was never part of our education system. Those in power know that the less we know about money, the more control they have over us. We work endlessly at our jobs, only to have "Them" take a chunk of our paycheck in taxes. Ever look at those taxes and wonder where they go? The powers that be decide what we the people supposedly need. The government and the banks! It's time to change that.

Death and Taxes, they say. Two certainties in life. But taxes aren't meant to be an oppressive burden. What if, you could create an endowment for yourself while you're alive AND upon your passing,could leave behind a legacy that empowers and uplifts your loved ones and your community? That would make life more purposeful and maybe, just maybe, death a little less daunting. Welcome to Social SecharityTM!

I first met Les Winston years ago during his radio program, "Funny Money." Admittedly, I wasn't paying much attention. But as fate would have it, our paths crossed again. And that's when it all started to make sense.

I've learned that having a great tax advisor is

crucial to saving money. And as for the taxes I do have to pay, I've shifted my perspective. Rather than seeing it as a burden, I now view it as voluntary giving out of love. But imagine a future where we get to choose where our tax money goes. No one in their right mind wants to financially support pointless wars and a monolithic bureaucracy. As our collective consciousness continues to grow, wars will diminish and bureaucracy will shrink. Our government will become more accountable and life on Earth will become happier.

excerpted from "Essays on Creating Reality Book 2" by Frederick Dodson.

Prepare to have your mind blown!

Chapter 1

The Financial Odyssey of Les Winston and Endow America Network Foundation

So, here we are, gathered around the campfire of fiscal responsibility, roasting marshmallows made of financial jargon. Today's tale revolves around Les Winston, the unsung hero of financial empowerment, and his merry band of financial wizards, The Endow America Network Foundation (EANF). Imagine a world where money matters are as thrilling as a Netflix series—well, this is it, and Les and EANF are the stars of the show.

Les Winston isn't your typical financial guru. He doesn't sport a three-piece suit or talk in a language that requires a secret decoder ring. No, Les is the guy you'd meet at a neighborhood barbecue, sharing tips on how to grow your savings while flipping burgers. His background is a patchwork quilt of real-life experiences, not just a resume listing fancy degrees and corporate conquests.

Picture this: Les Winston, a man on a mission to

liberate the masses from financial despair. With his commitment to financial empowerment, Les is like the Gandalf of money matters, waving his wand (or maybe a well-worn calculator) to make financial literacy accessible to all.

Now, let's talk about EANF – the Avengers of the financial realm. Armed with the mighty Tax Code 664, they're on a mission to make wealth-building the coolest party in town. They don't wear capes unless it's a fashion statement, but they do wield financial acumen with superhero-like precision. Their mission? To spread the gospel of Tax Code 664 far and wide, like financial missionaries of fiscal enlightenment.

Why Tax Code 664, you ask? Well, it's not your average tax code. It's the superhero among numbers, the chosen one destined to bring financial liberation. Les and EANF are here to unravel the mysteries of this magical code and make it the centerpiece of your financial feast.

Les Winston's journey is not a saga of suits and ties but a relatable yarn spun from the fabric of everyday life. He's been in the trenches, faced financial dragons, and emerged wiser and more determined to share his knowledge. Les isn't the guy who'll drone on about compound interest in monotone;

he's the storyteller who makes financial tales as riveting as a blockbuster movie.

EANF isn't your typical foundation. They're the rebels of financial education, challenging the norms and championing Tax Code 664. With Les Winston as their fearless leader, they're not just spreading awareness; they're creating a movement, a financial revolution that encourages everyone to take control of their money destinies.

Les and EANF might not wear capes, but they are the unsung heroes of the financial universe. Les brings humor and relatability to the table, making financial literacy a joyride instead of a snooze-fest. Meanwhile, EANF acts as the wizard's apprentice, passing on the knowledge of Tax Code 664 like a sacred torch.

In this financial odyssey, Les Winston and EANF are the sherpas guiding us through the treacherous terrain of money management. So, let's join them on this whimsical adventure where Tax Code 664 isn't just a bunch of numbers—it's the key to unlocking a world of financial possibilities. The journey may be filled with laughs, quirks, and aha moments, but one thing's for sure: by the end, you'll be equipped with the wisdom to navigate the financial landscape like a true money maestro.

C hapter 2
Les Winston's Vision: Tax Codes, High-Interest CDs, and Mom's Legacy

So, let me tell you about Les Winston – the man with a vision so sharp, you could cut through taxes with it. Picture this: Les, a financial wizard with a heart bigger than his calculator, navigating the labyrinth of Tax Code 664 and societal challenges.

Les's journey starts like a movie – with a backstory that's part heartwarming, part financial odyssey. His mother, born in war-torn Austria, witnessed her father's shooting, endured famine, and faced the worst living conditions war could muster. But then, like a beacon of hope, the United States intervened. With funds provided by Aunt Anna, Les's family sailed across the Atlantic, escaping the clutches of war.

And here's Les's mom, grateful as a cat with a bowl of cream. "They gave me comfort. They educated us, fed us, housed us. If not for the government, you wouldn't be here," she'd say. It's not just a financial tale; it's a saga of gratitude, a dance with life's ups and downs.

Fast forward to Les's family – hardworking, competitive, and high-fiving prosperity. His mother and Uncle Joe, engaged in a friendly duel, competing to secure the highest interest return on their CDs. Les chuckles at the memory, "She was able to accumulate over $1 million before her death at age 87. My brother and I couldn't change her thinking."

Now, Les wasn't just dealing with numbers; he was wrestling with a legacy. His mother, a saver and a hard worker, reveled in the "high return on a CD." Even in the face of financial wisdom from her financial planner sons, she stood her ground. "Taxes, schmaxes, I love the government," she'd proclaim.

The turning point – the painful check for over $400,000 written to the U.S. Treasury. "But, that's what mom wanted, and that's what we did." Les, the financial planner extraordinaire, couldn't convince his mother to change her mind. Giving to charity wasn't her thing, and her sentiment echoed through the ages. Les reflects, "A man convinced against his will is of the same opinion still."

He shares a poignant moment from an audience

presentation – an elderly woman leaving in protest. "How does he think the government will run?" she retorted. Les's experiences echo the sentiments of many around his mother's age, a generation where the government's role was cherished, not contested.

Les doesn't just talk about tax codes; he philosophizes about the informed and the uninformed. Quoting the Honorable Learned Hand, he emphasizes, "You have the right to reduce your taxes as much as legally possible." And yet, a double barrier looms – lack of information and, most importantly, the absence of charitable intent.

As Les wraps up his chapter, you can almost hear the collective nod of understanding. It's not just about tax codes; it's about gratitude, legacy, and the enduring tug-of-war between financial wisdom and personal beliefs. Les Winston isn't just a financial planner; he's a storyteller weaving tales of numbers, heart, and the complexities of human intent. And in this symphony of financial musings, Tax Code 664 takes center stage, playing a tune that harmonizes with the ebb and flow of life's financial journey.

C hapter 3
Social Secharity™ - A Comedy of Contributions

Alright, gather around, folks! I've got a tale for you, a story of innovation, generosity, and a touch of involuntary charity. Picture this: the grand entrance of Social Secharity, a proposed involuntary Charitable Remainder Trust (CRT), waltzing into the world of Social Security benefits like the belle of the ball.

Now, let me take you on a journey through the intricacies of Tax Code 664. It's not your typical bedtime story, but hey, who said tax codes can't be entertaining?

Imagine diving headfirst into the legal labyrinth of Tax Code 664. It's a maze, folks, but fear not – we're equipped with a blueprint of key provisions and a GPS tuned to the legal framework. This ain't your grandma's treasure hunt; it's a quest for understanding, sprinkled with humor and a touch of IRS-induced madness.

Now, let's navigate through the uncharted territories of key provisions. It's like decoding a secret language, but instead of ancient scrolls, we've got the IRS playbook. Brace yourselves for terms like "Charitable Remainder Trust" and "Federal Bond investment requirement." Sounds riveting, doesn't it? Well, grab your popcorn, because this is just the beginning.

Enter the world of various charitable remainder trusts, each with its own set of applications. It's like a buffet of financial choices, but instead of dishes, we've got CRUTs, CRATs, and the star of our show – the Social SecharityTM Charitable Remainder Trust (SCRUT). It's a mouthful, but hey, the more acronyms, the merrier!

Now, let's talk about the proposed masterpiece – Social Secharity. It's not just a trust; it's a grand scheme, a 50-year plan to secure Social Security benefits. Workers of all ages contributing a varying percentage into their individual 501(c)(3) fund managed under a parent donor advised fund (DAF). Confused? Don't worry, we all are.

During the phase-in period, the Social Security Trust Fund account would be balanced to cover any shortfalls by borrowing from the CRT accounts through a Federal Bond investment requirement. Imagine the Social Security Trust Fund doing a financial balancing act, borrowing from the CRT accounts like a magician pulling rabbits out of hats. It's a spectacle, folks, a financial circus where everyone's a performer.

This proposal aims to ensure the long-term sustainability of Social Security benefits while providing a secure and flexible retirement savings option for workers, contributing to a return to the American spirit of innovation and generosity.

So, there you have it – Tax Code 664 and the comedic opera of Social Secharity. It's not your everyday bedtime story, I know. But who said taxes couldn't be fun? Now, go forth, my friends, and navigate the financial maze with the wisdom of Tax Code 664 and the laughter of Social SecharityTM echoing in your ears.

C hapter 4
The Endow America Network Foundation's Quest for Knowledge and Policy Tweaks

In the world of financial acronyms and regulatory labyrinths, there emerges a hero in the form of the Endow America Network Foundation (EANF). Join me on this exhilarating journey as we explore EANF's ingenious initiatives, guided by the sagacious spirit of Charity.

Ah, the noble quest for enlightenment! Imagine EANF as the Gandalf of the financial realm, wielding educational campaigns like a wizard casting spells. But instead of magic wands, they use strategies – cunning, ingenious, and occasionally comical.

EANF dives headfirst into the tumultuous sea of financial illiteracy armed with strategies sharper than Excalibur. Picture this: Financial Literacy Workshops where participants don't just learn about Tax Code 664, but dance to a tax-themed rendition of "YMCA." It's a strategy to make learning stick, to turn tax code jargon into a catchy tune that echoes in the minds of participants long after the workshop ends.

EANF doesn't stop there. They've embraced the digital age like a teenager with a smartphone addiction. Webinars, podcasts, and YouTube tutorials transform complex financial concepts into bite-sized, digestible nuggets. It's like EANF is hosting the "Tax Code 664 Variety Show," where even the most mundane tax topics are presented with flair, and a hint of sarcasm.

Enter the Avengers of Financial Literacy – EANF collaborates with educational institutions and financial experts, creating a league of extraordinary educators. Universities become the battlegrounds where financial enlightenment fights the good fight against ignorance. Professors, armed with PowerPoint slides and charismatic charm, team up with EANF to conquer the minds of the young and old alike.

Imagine financial experts delivering TED Talks, not in stuffy boardrooms, but in the heart of communities. Picture a financial guru discussing the nuances of Tax Code 664 while sitting on a park bench, sipping coffee, and feeding pigeons. EANF brings financial literacy to the streets, turning it into a movement, a crusade against financial ignorance.

Now, let's talk about the unsung heroes, the Endowment Engineers – the eloquent voices and policy architects shaping the future.

We see Les Winston, the maestro of financial wisdom, taking center stage like a stand-up comedian at a financial comedy club. Public speaking engagements become a symphony of wit, charm, and financial enlightenment. Les, with a mic in one hand and a tax code in the other, weaves tales of Tax Code 664 like a troubadour singing ballads of financial freedom.

Media appearances become the canvas where EANF paints the masterpiece of financial literacy. Imagine Les on a late-night show, breaking down the complexities of tax codes with a sprinkle of humor. It's a performance that rivals Shakespearean dramas, with financial epiphanies replacing tragic soliloquies.

But EANF isn't just about words; they're the crusaders for policy changes and improvements related to Tax Code 664. Advocacy becomes their sword, cutting through bureaucratic red tape with finesse. Picture Les Winston storming into congressional hearings, armed not with aggression but with a PowerPoint presentation that rivals the most captivating TED Talks.

EANF becomes the voice in the ears of policymakers, the whisper that says, "Hey, let's tweak this tax code for the better." They advocate for changes that benefit individuals, communities, and the future Generation Alpha. It's not just about numbers; it's about creating a financial utopia where tax codes make sense and everyone can high-five prosperity.

In the grand theater of financial literacy, EANF takes the stage, armed with knowledge, charisma, and a commitment to making Tax Code 664 the hero in the story of financial enlightenment. As the curtain falls on this chapter, we're left with a sense of awe – EANF, the unsung heroes, fighting the good fight, one educational campaign and policy tweak at a time.

C hapter 5

Weaving Wealth, Tax Codes, and the Symphony of Community Impact

Welcome back, avid readers, to the culmination of our financial voyage, where the Endowment Engineers, led by Les Winston, weave through the intricate dance of Tax Code 664, crafting a symphony of community impact.

In the realm of wealth maximization through Tax Code 664, the Endowment Engineers, guided by Les Winston, emerge as the architects of strategic movements and harmonies.

Picture the Endowment Engineers, not in tutus but in tailored suits, coaching individuals through a ballet of trust assets. It's not just a numerical exercise; it's a precise performance where individuals gracefully navigate the complexities, seamlessly blending personal aspirations with charitable goals. The Endowment Engineers, the financial choreographers, guide this ballet with precision and finesse.

As we waltz through the financial dreamscape, the Endowment Engineers become dance partners, leading individuals through the intricate steps of balancing charitable and personal goals. The dance floor is Tax Code 664, where tax benefits waltz alongside personal aspirations. It's a sophisticated waltz, creating a masterpiece of financial harmony under the skilled direction of the Endowment Engineers.

Now, let's witness the financial alchemy of Tax Code 664 as the Endowment Engineers weave a tapestry of community impact through Charitable Remainder Trusts.

The Endowment Engineers, wielding metaphorical wands, reveal the secrets of how CRTs orchestrate a symphony of prosperity for local communities. It's not just financial impact; it's a harmonious symphony echoing through the streets. The Endowment Engineers, the conductors, guide this symphony, with each note representing a community project funded by the financial magic of CRTs.

In this enchanting world, community projects funded through CRTs become not just examples but financial narratives turned reality. The Endowment Engineers, the storytellers, share tales of community centers, scholarships, and revitalized parks. It's not just about wealth accumulation; it's about turning financial dreams into tangible community improvements.

And now, the grand vision of the Endowment Engineers unfolds. Picture 538 Congressional district foundations, each with 500,000 family foundations – a financial utopia where family foundations, administered at the CDF level, shape the transformation of communities. National administrators, including United Way, NHF, NCF, NFI/CCF, MDRT, Renaissance, Fidelity, SEI, and more, ensure this vision becomes a tangible reality.

The financial alchemy extends to donor-advised fund supporting organizations, who, like financial maestros, become qualified administrators. They categorize accounts by areas of service, creating a grand exchange index for charity. The federal government, playing the role of a benevolent overseer, intervenes only in cases of misfeasance, ensuring funds are redirected or utilized in national disasters.

As the curtain falls on this chapter, we're left with a sense of wonder and anticipation. Wealth building,

Tax Code 664, and community impact – it's not just a financial journey; it's an eloquent expedition into a future where financial dreams and community aspirations perform a nuanced dance of prosperity. And so, the financial symphony continues, with the Endowment Engineers conducting the orchestra of wealth, tax codes, and community enchantment.

C hapter 6
Eliminating Problems in America

Like a troupe of awkward dancers, the problems in America, too, sway in unison, synchronized by the rhythm of socioeconomic disparities. Who are we to stand idly by and merely observe this melancholic performance?

Let's talk about Tax Code 664, the unsung hero, the quiet custodian of fairness. It's a little like the underappreciated youngest child, doing its part to reduce inequalities. And what a job it does! Like a skilled gardener pruning the branches of wealth disparity, Tax Code 664 trims away overgrown privilege, redistributing it to the undernourished roots below.

But let's not forget the real victims here - the disadvantaged communities. They stand outside the warm glow of economic prosperity, noses pressed against the glass, watching the feast within. And, in an ironic twist worthy of a Greek tragedy, they are often the ones hardest hit by social and economic impact. Yet, like dandelions sprouting through cracks in a sidewalk, they persist.

Next, we turn to the intriguing game of financial musical chairs that is wealth redirection. Imagine, if you will, money flowing like a river from the mountains of affluence into the valleys of need. The goal? To support critical social initiatives. Like a lifeline thrown to a drowning man, this redirected wealth can be the difference between sinking and survival.

But, of course, it's not just about survival. It's about growth. It's about solving problems. It's about addressing pressing issues through charitable giving. Think of it as a societal band-aid, applied liberally and often. Because, as we know, a problem ignored is a problem doubled. So, let us not shy away from these issues. Let us face them head-on, with Charity and compassion, as we strive to eliminate problems in America.

Education is often touted as the key to success, but for many in America, access to quality education can be a significant barrier. This issue disproportionately affects disadvantaged communities and perpetuates the cycle of poverty and inequality.

But there are solutions within our reach. By investing in programs that provide equal educational opportunities, we can level the playing field and give every child a chance to succeed. This not only benefits individuals but also has a positive impact on society as a whole. A well-educated population leads to economic growth, innovation, and a stronger sense of community.

As we strive towards eliminating problems in America, let us not forget the crucial role that education plays. By providing equal access to quality education, we can create a more equal and prosperous society for all.

Addressing socioeconomic disparities, funding social programs, and promoting access to education are crucial steps in eliminating problems in America. It is not enough to simply observe and acknowledge these issues; it is our responsibility as a society to actively work towards solutions. By coming together with compassion, generosity, and a determination for change, we can create a better future for all Americans. Let us not forget the power that lies within our hands to shape a more equitable and just society. The performance may be melancholic now, but with our collective efforts, we can create a symphony of progress and hope for the generations to come. So let us dance towards a brighter tomorrow.

C hapter 7
Retirement Income for Generation Alpha - A Fresh Approach with Tax Code 664

Retirement is often portrayed as a time for relaxation, enjoying the rewards of hard work. We all long for peaceful sunsets, leisurely tea conversations, or even virtual golf. But can Generation Alpha achieve this idyllic vision?

Generation Alphas, the hologram-loving, hyper-connected, Gen Z successors born between 2010 and 2025, are now approaching an unusual dichotomy — they must consider saving for their AI-assisted sunset years while barely out of adolescence. A sobering thought. It's as if, in preparing for a future singularity, they're losing the present.

I see them scratching their heads, pondering 401(k)s, IRAs, and the elusive stock market. It's like trying to explain quantum physics to a cat. And let's not even get started on the rollercoaster of Social Security. Generation Alpha is facing a retirement puzzle where the pieces keep changing shapes, and the picture on the box is a blurry meme.

But fear not, our future Alpha retirees. Underneath our monstrous tax code, buried somewhere between exciting discussions around ordinary and necessary expenses, lies a beacon of hope, Tax Code 664.

"Tax Code 664. The very name sounds like it belongs to an inscrutable bureaucracy or an unpopular droid from 'Star Wars'. But trust me when I say it could be your ticket to sipping holographic champagne on your interplanetary cruise retirement."

Tax Code 664, or Social SecharityTM, boasts significant perks for retirement income generation. Without going all 'Star Trek' on you, let me explain its few fascinating aspects.

This fringe of the legal code allows for the establishment of charitable remainder trusts, or CRTs. Simply put, you donate assets into a trust— you get a tax deduction as a cherry on top. The trust then sells your assets, bubbles up your set annual income, and upon your departure to the other side of the galaxy, the remainder goes to a registered charity.

What's not to like? You get a reliable income stream

throughout retirement, an attractive tax deduction, and the peace of knowing that anything leftover will go to a worthy cause. Imagine a retirement where the only 'bucket list' you worry about is the one full of virtual beach holidays or inter-galactic safaris, not medical bills or grocery expenses. That's what Tax Code 664 can do for your retirement dreams.

There you have it, Alphas. A new approach to retirement planning. Reconsidering how you save and putting trust in something named after a number and a few unremarkable letters. Welcome to Tax Code 664. Welcome to the future of retirement income.

C hapter 8
The Perils and Pitfalls of Tax Code 664

Welcome, my discerning readers, to the chapter where we unmask the challenges and adjustments that come with the territory of Tax Code 664. Once again, I'm your guide, Charity. Buckle up for a ride through the potential drawbacks and risks that lurk behind the curtain of financial wizardry.

As we delve into the financial theatre, Tax Code 664 takes center stage, donning a mask of reliability. But, let's be honest—no hero's journey is without a few stumbles and pratfalls. Generation Alpha, armed with the wisdom of Tax Code 664, faces challenges that unfold like scenes in a Shakespearean play.

Picture our protagonist, Tax Code 664, facing unexpected twists, a comedy of errors where the punchlines are tax regulations and the plot thickens with market fluctuations. It's a lesson in humility, a reminder that even the most reliable financial sidekick has its quirks.

"Ah, Tax Code 664, you're like that friend who means well but always finds a way to complicate a simple plan," I chuckle. Our lessons start here, in the belly of the comedy beast. Generation Alpha learns that even with the best intentions, financial plans can take unexpected turns. Tax Code 664 becomes the quirky character in this financial sitcom, teaching lessons through laughter and a few forehead-slapping moments.

Now, how does our protagonist respond to these challenges? Tax Code 664 becomes the wise mentor, offering strategies for adaptation to the evolving needs of Generation Alpha. It's a dance of flexibility and resilience, a ballet of financial adjustments in the face of uncertainty.

"Think of Tax Code 664 as a financial MacGyver," I muse. "Always ready to fashion a solution out of a paperclip and some tax regulations."

As we explore these strategies, it becomes clear that Tax Code 664 isn't just a set of rules; it's a living document that responds to the ever-changing financial landscape. It's a financial chameleon, blending into the background when needed and emerging as a guiding light when uncertainty looms.

In this comedy of financial errors and tragedies, Tax Code 664 teaches Generation Alpha the art of adaptation. It's not about avoiding pitfalls altogether but learning to pirouette through them with grace. The financial stage is ever-changing, and Tax Code 664 becomes the seasoned actor, adjusting its lines to fit the script of economic evolution.

As the curtain falls on the potential drawbacks and risks, Generation Alpha steps into the spotlight, armed not just with Tax Code 664 but with the resilience to face the financial stage with confidence. The lessons learned become the script for a financial comedy that transcends challenges, turning potential tragedies into moments of growth and adaptation.

And so, dear readers, we conclude this chapter with a nod to the unpredictable nature of finance. Tax Code 664, our quirky protagonist, continues to guide Generation Alpha through the financial theatre, reminding us that in the grand performance of wealth-building, adaptation is the standing ovation. Cheers to Tax Code 664, the maestro of financial evolution!

C hapter 9
The Spiritual Symphony: Harmonizing Wealth and Abundance in the New World

Greetings, fellow seekers of both financial prowess and spiritual enlightenment! As we embark on this whimsical yet profound journey into Chapter 9, I, your enthusiastic guide, invite you to explore the sacred dance between wealth-building and spiritual abundance. Buckle up for a delightful ride through the realms of Dodson's generosity, Ragusin's vision, and the fusion of spiritual wisdom with financial planning.

Imagine this: a cozy little cafe where dollars and divinity engage in delightful banter over a cup of celestial coffee. We kick off our exploration with the introduction to spiritual wealth—a realm where the currency of kindness holds just as much weight as the almighty dollar.

What if I told you that financial prosperity and spiritual abundance are dance partners, twirling in perfect synchrony? In this introduction, we unravel the threads that weave together the spiritual tapestry of wealth-building. It's not just about dollars and cents; it's about the cents of spirituality.

Enter the divine tango of spiritual principles and financial abundance. It's a dance floor where generosity waltzes with prosperity, and charitable remainder trusts perform a ballet of benevolence. This fusion isn't just a harmonious melody—it's the soundtrack of a spiritually affluent life.

In this section, we delve into Frederick Dodson's insights on the spiritual significance of giving. Picture generosity as a virtuoso violinist in the orchestra of spiritual acts. We explore how charitable remainder trusts join this symphony, playing their part in creating a crescendo of abundance.

Now, let's step into Kristen Ragusin's vision—a world where scarcity is but a distant memory, and abundance is shared for the greater good. Charitable endeavors become not just acts of kindness but pathways to spiritual fulfillment. It's the end of scarcity and the birth of a new era, where prosperity is a shared banquet.

But wait, there's a whisper in the cosmic winds—a thought that lingers like the fragrance of incense in a sacred space. Ragusin envisions a money revolution, a seismic shift where the currency of the heart supersedes the mere exchange of bills. The revolution isn't just financial; it's a spiritual awakening, a collective realization that money can be a force for good.

"Money is not the root of all evil," Ragusin declares. "It's a tool for transformation. A tool we wield with love and intention to create a world where abundance is not a privilege but a birthright."

I imagine Dodson and Ragusin sharing a cup of cosmic tea, discussing their shared vision of a world united in abundance. We explore the spiritual essence of collective prosperity, where unity and oneness become the guiding principles of this brave new world.

In this segment, we break free from the shackles of scarcity thinking. It's a journey of overcoming limiting beliefs through spiritual practices, encouraging a shift towards positive, abundance-oriented thinking. The stage is set for a grand transformation—a spiritual revolution against the tyranny of lack.

Now, let's bring the spiritual wisdom into the practical realm of financial decisions. It's not just about balancing checkbooks; it's about balancing material wealth with spiritual well-being. The financial dance becomes a sacred ballet, choreographed with the steps of conscious decision-making.

As our journey nears its end, we cast a spiritual gaze into the future. What might America look and feel like in 2050 through the lens of spiritual consciousness? The chapter concludes with a tantalizing vision of a more harmonious and prosperous society—a testament to the power of blending wealth with spiritual abundance.

And so, dear readers, we bid adieu to Chapter 9 —a whimsical expedition into the heart of wealth and spirituality. May your pockets be full, and your souls even fuller as you carry forth the lessons of this spiritual symphony into the grand ballroom of life. Cheers to dollars, divinity, Ragusin's money revolution, and the dance of abundance!

C hapter 10
The Synthesis of Spirituality and Wealth

So you want to know the secret sauce, the ultimate two-birds-one-stone strategy? Well, buckle up, folks, because we're about to take a detour from the mundane and dive head-first into the extraordinary union of spirituality and wealth.

First things first, let's be clear. No, we're not talking about manifesting a million-dollar check from the Universe. (Though, hey, if that's your jam, more power to you!) We're addressing the transformative power that comes from aligning spiritual principles with financial practices. Imagine for a second, your money habits, and your spiritual beliefs, sitting together, sipping tea, in perfect harmony. A bit of fiscal Zen, anyone?

But hey, I hear you ask, "How can one achieve this mythical balance?" Well, dear reader, it starts by embracing a holistic approach to wealth creation. Think of it as a promising ticket to a spiritually fulfilling future. And no, you don't need to be a yogi millionaire or a Wall Street guru for this. Just a regular person, like you and I, willing to embrace a richer perspective (pun intended!).

Let's bring in the big guns now - tax code 664 and Social SecharityTM. Sounds dull, right? But trust me, when applied correctly, these can be your next best friends. These tools allow you to give charitably, reduce taxes, and oh, did I mention, feel pretty darn good about yourself? It's like having your cake, eating it too, and not feeling guilty about the calories!

So, here's to the brave souls embarking on this journey to build wealth and support a cause they believe in. Cheers to the synthesis of spirituality and wealth, may it prove to be your guiding North Star. Just remember, it's not just about adding more zeroes to your bank account, but also about infusing meaning into those numbers. Because at the end of the day, isn't that what true wealth is all about?

C hapter 11
Les Winston and EANF: The Wizards of Wealth and Kindness

Greetings, you savvy readers! Here we are, at Chapter 11 – the juicy meat of this financial feast. I'm Charity, here to guide you through a reflection on Les Winston and the Endow America Network Foundation (EANF), where wealth-building meets witty wisdom.

First things first, let's talk about gratitude. Picture Les Winston as the magician pulling dollars out of a hat, and EANF as the grand wizard's wand making financial dreams come true. We're not just saying thanks; we're throwing a financial gratitude party!

"Les Winston, the man who turns tax codes into blueprints, deserves a standing ovation," I exclaim. But in all seriousness, gratitude is in order for their unwavering dedication to promoting opportunities that turn pocket change into prosperity.

Now, let's delve into the magic show that's

the positive transformation in individuals and communities. It's like Les and EANF are the financial wizards, turning financial struggles into success stories and poverty into prosperity.

"It's not just about balancing checkbooks; it's about the alchemy of turning cents into celebrations," I joke. Recognition is due for the way they've sprinkled their fairy dust of financial empowerment, making communities sparkle with newfound abundance.

Now, imagine Route 664 as the yellow brick road leading to the Emerald City of financial literacy. Les, EANF, philanthropists, and change makers are all on board, making this journey a whimsical radio extravaganza.

Let's emphasize the importance of financial literacy through our radio station. It's not just a station; it's a musical cruise through the seas of human kindness. We connect with philanthropists, change makers, and play tunes that make you feel like a financial superhero.

"Because who needs a superhero cape when you've got financial wisdom on the airwaves?" I quip. The Route 664 webcast and radio show are the Hogwarts

Express to Money Hogwarts, teaching us spells like "Accio Prosperity" and "Expecto Patronum for Financial Woes."

As we wrap up, let's encourage more collaboration and innovation. It's not just about riding the wave of financial literacy; it's about building a surfboard of change-making collaboration.

"Because when change makers unite, it's like a superhero crossover event," I chuckle. The future is prosperous when we continue to collaborate, innovate, and maybe throw in a dance move or two. The financial boogie of the future is awaiting its next chart-topping hit.

C

hapter 12

2050: A Utopia of Wealth, Thriving Communities, and Social Harmony

Hello, dear readers! Charity here, your guide into the utopian landscape of 2050, where our communities are thriving, our wealth is soaring, and social harmony reigns supreme. Join me as we explore the dazzling legacy of decades of Tax Code 664 usage.

Picture this: a world where Tax Code 664 is the hero, quietly accumulating wealth over the decades. The cumulative impact is nothing short of extraordinary. Thanks to the strategic usage of this tax code, we've witnessed a financial metamorphosis that has catapulted our nation into an era of abundance.

Now, let's take a stroll down memory lane for a historical perspective. Back in the days leading up to 2020, wealth distribution was a wobbly tightrope act, and societal progress often felt like an elusive dream. The shift to Tax Code 664 wasn't just a financial revolution; it was a societal evolution that rewrote the script of progress.

Imagine communities as vibrant ecosystems, thriving under the benevolent shade of Charitable Remainder Trusts (CRTs). Thanks to these financial guardians, schools, hospitals, youth services, roads and cultural amenities have not just survived but blossomed. The benefits of CRTs have been the nourishing rain for our societal garden.

Opportunities knock louder in 2050. The strategic usage of Tax Code 664 has opened doors and windows, creating increased opportunities for everyone. Our quality of life has seen a marked improvement, like a grand symphony of progress playing in the background.

With improved economic conditions, societal problems have taken a backseat. Picture a symphony where reduced poverty, enhanced education, and improved healthcare play in perfect harmony. Tax Code 664 has orchestrated a melody of prosperity that has silenced discordant notes. Hallelujah!

Let's gaze into the crystal ball of optimism. In this envisioned America, equity is not just a word; it's a way of life. Economic conditions have been the great equalizer, paving the way for a society where everyone has a fair shot at success. It's a vision where harmony isn't just a fleeting moment but a perpetual state of being.

We tip our hats to Les Winston and EANF – the maestros of this financial symphony. May their legacy echo through wallets and communities alike. Here's to gratitude, financial literacy on the airwaves, and the ever-evolving dance of collaboration and innovation.

As we bid adieu to this journey into 2050, let's carry the spirit of Tax Code 664 with us. It's not just about financial prosperity; it's about creating a legacy of abundance for generations to come. Cheers to a future where wealth, thriving communities, and social harmony dance hand in hand. Until next time, stay whimsical, my friends!

About the Author

Wanda Myles, a versatile professional with an unwavering passion for creative expression and social impact, is making waves in the industry. As the Creative Director at SocialSecharity.org, she is at the forefront of driving the country towards economic well-being through charitable wealth.

With an infectious personality and exceptional production skills, Myles has become a standout in the broadcasting industry. Her colorful career includes roles as a Program Director, Host, and Producer at Salem Media Group and National Public Radio's WLRN. As a sought-after voice talent, she brings a captivating warmth and unwavering professionalism to every project.

Not content with just audio, Myles is also a skilled audio and video producer, consistently exceeding expectations and creating exceptional content. Her dedication to her craft and commitment to excellence shine through in all her work.

Beyond her professional achievements, Myles is a true community member and benefactor. Committed to spreading kindness and making a difference wherever she goes, she is a beacon of inspiration for those around her.

https:/route664.com

https://www.facebook.com/wandaPmyles

https://socialsecharity.org/home

Made in the USA
Columbia, SC
24 December 2024